ANCIENT GREECE
Activity Book

Author	Mary Jo Keller
Editor	Deneen Celecia
Cover Design	Wendy Loreen
Page Design	Linda Milliken

About the Author

Mary Jo Keller attended The College of New Rochelle in New Rochelle, New York and William and Mary in Williamsburg, Virginia. For the past thirteen years she has worked designing and implementing programs for various youth organizations such as the Boy Scouts of America and the Girl Scouts of America. She has also directed summer day camps for eight years.

METRIC CONVERSION CHART

Refer to this chart when metric conversions are not found within the activity.

¼ tsp. =	1 ml	350° F =	180° C
½ tsp. =	2 ml	375° F =	190° C
1 tsp. =	5 ml	400° F =	200° C
1 Tbsp. =	15 ml	425° F =	216° C
¼ cup =	60 ml	1 inch =	2.54 cm
⅓ cup =	80 ml	1 foot =	30 cm
½ cup =	125 ml	1 yard =	91 cm
1 cup =	250 ml	1 mile =	1.6 km
1 oz. =	28 g		
1 lb. =	.45 kg		

EP062 • ©1995 Edupress, Inc. • P.O. Box 883 • Dana Point, CA 92629
www.edupressinc.com

ISBN 1-56472-062-4
Printed in USA

Table of Contents

Literature List

- **The Shining Stars:
Greek Legends of the Zodiac**
by G. Vautier; Cambridge 1981. (4-6)
The Greek legends of the origin of each
sign of the zodiac are retold.

- **Greeks**
by Rachel Wright; Watts LB 1993. (3-6)
Presents the everyday life of ancient
Greeks, their clothing and their buildings.

- **Greece in Pictures**
by Lerner LB 1992. (5-6)
Through photos, maps, charts and concise
text, the land and people of Greece are
introduced.

- **Greece**
by R. Stein; Childrens LB 1985. (5-7)
Everyday life, history, culture and
geographic features are covered.

- **Cooking the Greek Way**
by Lynne Villios; Lerner LB 1984. (5-8)
The young cook is introduced to the
cuisine of Greece.

- **The Fables of Aesop**
by Aesop; Schocken 1966. (4-5)
Eighty-two fables considered among
Aesop's most familiar and effective.

- **Aesop and Company**
by Barbara Bader; Houghton 1991. (4-6)
A background book that traces the origins
of Aesop's fables and their use through the
centuries.

- **In Ancient Greece**
by Philip Sauvain; Macmillan 1992. (3-6)
A survey of life in classical Greece,
including the home, theater and warfare.

- **The Sorcerer's Apprentice:
A Greek Fable**
by Marianna Mayer; Bantam 1989. (3-5)
An apprentice creates problems when
magic he produces gets out of control.

- **The Children's Homer:
The Adventures of Odysseus and
the Tale of Troy**
by Padraic Colum; Macmillan 1982. (4-6)
The engrossing tales of Homer.

- **The Parthenon**
by Susan Woodford; Macmillan 1992. (5)
History and structure of the Parthenon and
a description of religion of ancient Greece.

- **Alexander the Great**
by Maureen Ash; Childrens 1991. (4-6)
An account of the Macedonian hero whose
empire stretched from Europe to Asia.

- **Ancient Greece**
by Daniel Cohen; Doubleday 1990. (4-6)
A brisk introduction to ancient Greece in
an oversized picture essay.

- **The Golden Days of Greece**
by Olivia Coolidge; Harper LB 1990. (5-6)
The culture and everyday life of Athens
and Sparta.

- **Science in Ancient Greece**
by Kathleen Gay; Watts LB 1988. (5-6)
A look at scientific achievements of long
ago, including advancements in math.

- **The Trojan Horse**
by Warwick Hutton; Macmillan 1992. (4)
The old story of the Trojan horse is told,
this time from the viewpoint of ordinary
people.

Ancient Greek World

Historical Aid

European civilization started in Greece more than 2,000 years ago. In those days, Greece controlled most of the land bordering the Mediterranean and Black Seas.

To the Greeks of the 5th century B.C., the world consisted of the Mediterranean Sea and the land around it. Herodotus was a famous historian and mapmaker. He was known as the "Father of History". He traveled throughout the civilized world in the mid-400s B.C. making maps and recording what he learned about other civilizations.

The Greeks believed the Mediterranean Sea stretched westward to the gardens of the Hesperides. This is where the sun god Helios landed his golden chariot every evening. He was born in a golden cup in his palace in the east. The next morning he drove his fiery chariot across the sky giving light to gods and mortals every day.

Project

Make a map and learn about modern map-making.

Materials

• Map drawn by Herodotus (below)

• Modern map of the world

• Neighborhood map (available in the phone book or from a real estate broker)

• Paper

• Pencils

Directions

1. Compare the map of the world drawn by Herodotus to a map of the world as it currently exists.

2. Have the students draw a map of what they think their neighborhood looks like. Have them compare their drawing to an actual map of the area.

3. Discuss the equipment modern mapmakers use to make their work so accurate, i.e. satellites and computers.

Time Line

Historical Aid

The Minoan culture was the first major civilization in the Greek world. It arose on the island of Crete about 3000 B.C. The development of Greek civilization began about 2000 B.C. when small farming villages were founded in Greece. This culture, called the Mycenaean culture, prospered on the Greek mainland from about 1600 to 1200 B.C. Greece's Dark Age lasted from 1200 to 800 B.C. In 776 B.C., the first Olympic games took place. In 490 and 479 B.C. the Greeks twice defeated Persian armies. The greatest art was produced during the Golden Age of Greece, 447 to 431 B.C. Sparta defeated Athens in the Peloponnesian War that lasted from 431 to 404 B.C. In 338 B.C., Philip II of Macedonia conquered the Greeks. Alexander the Great conquered most of the territory from Egypt to India in the years from 334 to 326 B.C. He built Greek cities and introduced the Greek culture wherever he ruled. In 323 B.C., Alexander the Great died and the Helenistic age began. Greece was conquered by the Romans in 146 B.C.

Project

Chart and illustrate the history of the ancient Greek empire.

Materials

• White butcher paper
• Pencils, marking pens or crayons
• Ruler

Directions

1. Explain the terms "time line" and "B.C."

2. Cut a long length of butcher paper.

3. Draw a line lengthwise across the paper. Mark the year 43 B.C. to the far right on the line. Using the Historical Aid above, mark the other important years in Greece's early history.

4. Illustrate the events beneath the time line.

Democracy in Athens

Historical Aid

The government of the city of Athens was a democracy—the people held the ruling power. The citizens met in a single assembly called the *ecclesia*. It was at these meetings that the people voted for laws and directed the magistrates who were chosen by lot to govern the city. If a magistrate did a poor job, he could be banished from the city for ten years! This procedure was called *ostracism* and we still use the same word today to mean banishment.

Any citizen had the right to speak in the ecclesia. The speaker would place a wreath of myrtle on his head. He was allowed a certain amount of time in which to speak. His time was measured by a *clepsydra* or water clock. He had to finish speaking before all the water ran from one *amphora* (pottery jar) into the other.

Project

Make a water clock. Use the water clock to keep time for a short speech.

Materials

- Two large empty cans of the same size
- Clock or watch with second hand
- Can opener
- Water

Directions

1. Make a small opening on the bottom edge of one can as illustrated.

2. Arrange the cans on a step or box so that the can with the hole is above the other can. Add water to the top can. Time how long it takes for the top can to empty. The time can be adjusted by adding or draining some water.

3. Pretend the class is a group of citizens at an ecclesia. Take turns speaking about "What I Remember Most About Ancient Greece" until the water clock runs out. To "reset" for the next student, simply pour the water from the bottom can back into the top can!

Foot Soldiers

Historical Aid

Each Greek city-state had its own army. Sometimes the states fought each other and sometimes they fought together against a foreign enemy. Athens, Sparta and Thebes had the strongest armies in Greece.

Foot soldiers were called *hoplites* because the Greek word for the round shields they carried was *hoplon*. These soldiers fought with two-edged swords and long wooden spears with metal points. Their armor consisted of a bronze breastplate, a helmet and "greaves" made of metal or leather to protect the soldier's legs. Sometimes a fringed leather apron would be attached to the bottom of a hoplite's shield to protect his legs. Hoplites fought in a block or phalanx formation consisting of about eight lines of soldiers. They all moved in step to the music of a pipe.

Project

Make a "leather apron" similar to the ones used by the hoplites on their shields.

Materials

- Large paper bags (grocery bags)
- Crayons
- Scissors
- Water

Directions

1. Cut down the seam of the paper bag and cut off the bottom. Crush and crumple the bag. Dip it in water, then smooth it out to dry.

2. When dry, cut the bag into an apron shape as shown, remembering to include the fringe.

3. Color with crayons. A popular design used in ancient Grecian times was one large eye.

7

Warships

Historical Aid

The Greeks were excellent shipbuilders. They built trading ships and ships to protect their long coastline from attack. Athens was the main naval power and many warships were built at her docks.

An example of a fast warship is the *trireme* (trī´ rēm). The fronts of these boats were made to look like sea monsters with a magic eye to ward off bad luck. Attached to the front of the boat was a sharp metal spike which was used as a ram to pierce the side of an enemy ship. One hundred and seventy oarsmen sat in three rows on each side of the boat. Their oars were different lengths depending on the height of the rower's seat. The rowers on the top level had to pull an oar that was ten feet long! The men rowed in time to flute music. In a battle, these strong men would row very fast to build up speed, pull in their oars and break off the oars of the enemy ship as they sailed past.

tape together here

Project

Design the prow of a Greek warship. Make a scenic picture of a trireme sailing on the Mediterranean Sea.

Directions

1. Make a copy of the trireme ship pattern for each student.

2. Tear the tissue paper into narrow strips. Lay them across the paper and brush down with starch. Mix some green strips with the blues to look like sea water.

3. Color, cut out and tape together the two halves of the warship. Don't forget to make the magic eye on the front of the ship. Glue to the sea to make the ship "sail".

Materials

- Blue and green tissue paper
- White construction paper
- Starch
- Paintbrush
- Trireme pattern, below
- Scissors
- Crayons or colored pencils
- Glue
- Tape

tape together here

Agora

Historical Aid

Ancient Greece was divided into very small independent states that consisted of a town and the surrounding farmland. These were called city-states. There was an open space at the center of each town called the *agora*. The word agora originally meant "meeting". The word came to mean "town center" because the men gathered there to discuss the important matters of the city-state.

The agora was surrounded by the main buildings of the city such as the law courts, army headquarters and the mint. The area was also used as the marketplace and was always crowded with shoppers and merchants. Farmers, bakers, cheese makers and fishermen displayed their wares in market stalls. Slaves could be purchased on a special day each month. Nearby were the workshops where many goods such as pots, sandals and jewelry were made.

Project

Recreate an ancient Greek marketplace in the classroom.

Materials

- Large towels or blankets
- Shopping baskets
- Bracelets (page 38) for jewelers to sell
- Articles to "sell" from following page
- Bread (page 40-41) or pita bread for bakers to sell

Directions

1. The class can make items for the market. Have the students bring a basket from home to hold their purchases. There were no paper bags available at the agora!

2. On market day, push the desks aside to make the marketplace. Some vendors had stalls to sell from, others spread out blankets. Use desks covered with blankets for stalls, or spread out blankets or towels on the floor.

3. Divide students into farmers, potters, metalworkers, traders, bakers, jewelers and sandal makers. Have them take turns shopping and minding their wares.

POTTER

Greek lamps looked like Aladdin's lamp, but they sometimes had two or more spouts!

Materials: clay, water

Directions:

1. Roll clay into a ball half the size of a tennis ball. Push your thumbs into clay, pinch and press clay into lamp shape.
2. Make two clay coils. Form one into a circle for the lamp's base. Make a handle from the other coil. Attach these coils by moistening them with a little bit of water.

SANDAL MAKER

Athenian women had their sandals custom-made from wooden soles and soft leather.

Materials: heavy cardboard, pencil, scissors, fabric strips or plastic grocery bags, hole punch

Directions:

1. Have the sandal maker trace the outline of his customer's foot onto the cardboard. Cut out. Punch holes in the sole as shown.
2. Cut fabric into three strips 3" x 36" (7.5 x 90 cm). Lace one piece of fabric through the holes as if lacing a sneaker. Attach the remaining pieces by tying them to the ends of the first piece. To wear, place foot under the laced part. Wrap strips around the leg to knee and tie.

FARMER

Barley is unfamiliar to many people today, but was a staple in the Greek diet.

Materials: nuts, carrots, grapes, dates, cheese, barley, celery, baskets or terra-cotta pots

Directions:

1. Arrange food in baskets or in pots.
2. After "shop-ping," celery, carrots and barley can be used in recipes on pages 40-41.

MERCHANTS

Traders imported items such as wheat, wood, mineral ores and refined metals, silks and fabric dyes from around the known world to sell at the agora. Make imported "silk" headbands to sell.

Materials: fabric, scissors, crayons

Directions:

1. Cut the fabric into lengths about 2" x 36" (5 x 90 cm).
2. Decorate with a Grecian "key" design.

METAL WORKERS

Craftsmen fashioned the pins that were used to fasten the Greeks' garments.

Materials: tagboard, scissors, toothpicks, aluminum foil, safety pins or pin backs, hot glue gun or tape

Directions:

1. Cut tagboard into circles about 1½" (3.75 cm) in diameter. Cover with foil.
2. Gently emboss designs into the foil with a toothpick.
3. Tape a safety pin to back or use hot glue to attach a pin back.

Festival

Historical Aid

Each city-state had a patron god and every year the people held a festival to honor their special god or goddess.

Athens' patron was the goddess Athena. Every summer her festival, called the *Panathenaea*, began with a relay torch race. The winner lit the sacred fire on Athena's altar. At dawn of the following day, a procession began with girls carrying cups and incense burners. Behind them came white oxen, water carriers and musicians. A decorated cart carried a new embroidered robe called a *peplos* for Athena's statue. At the end of the procession marched the priests, officials and townspeople. The oxen were sacrificed and roasted. The celebration continued for two days with feasting, dancing, singing, poetry competitions and games.

Project

Have a relay torch race like the ones held by the citizens of Athens centuries ago.

Materials

- Red, yellow and orange construction paper
- Paper towel tube
- Aluminum foil
- Scissors
- Masking tape

Directions

1. Cut the construction paper into strips as shown. One at a time, attach the strips on the masking tape as you wrap the tape around the tube. The colors should alternate.

2. Have a relay race. Divide the students into teams. Spread out the team members along the race track. The first runner holds the torch. When the race begins, he or she runs to the next player and passes the torch. Racers continue running and passing the torch until the last player crosses the finish line. That player's team wins!

Education

A boy growing up in Sparta would have a very different kind of education than his friend in Athens. In Sparta, physical fitness was more important than anything. In their state boarding schools, boys learned endurance, discipline and obedience. They became excellent soldiers.

Every boy in Athens had to learn a trade, but there were no laws about school. If a family could afford private school, their sons would learn to read, write, count with an abacus, play a stringed instrument called a *lyre* and recite poetry. Students spent the afternoons exercising in the gymnasium. Older boys either became an apprentice or studied with traveling teachers called *Sophists*.

Project

Make an abacus and practice showing numbers.

Directions

1. Carefully cut slits in the box lid.

2. Insert ten brads into each column. Experiment with showing different numbers on the abacus and see if your friends can decipher them.

How to use the abacus:

The column on the right is the ones column. Each brad has a value of one. The next column to the left is the tens column. Each brad on this column has a value of ten. The third column to the left is the hundreds column and each brad has a value of one hundred. The fourth column up is the thousands column. Each brad on this column has a value of one thousand.

You start with all the brads at the bottom, towards you. As you work, you push one or more brads to the top, away from you.

Suppose you want to show the number 1,352. Push up one brad in thousands column (1,000); push up three brads in hundreds column (300); push up five brads in tens column (50); and push up two brads in ones column (2).

Materials

• Brass brads
• Shoebox lid
• Scissors

Physical Fitness

Historical Aid

Physical fitness was very important to the ancient Greeks. They believed that a fit and healthy body was just as important as an educated mind. Men and boys would spend part of every day at the gymnasium.

In the city-state of Sparta, seven-year-old boys were sent to camp to begin their training to become soldiers and athletes. They were taught physical skills rather than mental ones. At age eleven, their training became even harder. The boys were deliberately kept hungry and their only clothing was a thin cloak, even in winter. They would rub themselves with snow and bathe in the icy river.

Sparta was the only city-state where girls were treated as the equals of boys. The girls were trained to be strong and independent. They learned to throw a discus and javelin, and run a footrace.

Project

Excercise and running were part of the daily life of a Spartan youth. Practice these skills.

Materials

• Large field or playground

Directions

1. Warm up by slowly jogging in place for two minutes.

2. Practice doing some jumping jacks, sit-ups and push-ups.

3. Run around the perimeter of the field or playground.

Sports

Sports competitions were popular in all the city-states of ancient Greece. Athletes trained from the time they were children to participate in the events. Small towns held competitions and athletes would travel from all over Greece to participate in the great sanctuaries at Olympia and Delphi.

Wrestling was a popular sport, as was *pancatium*, a combination of mud wrestling and boxing. Other favorite sports included javelin and discus throwing. A discus could weigh up to eight and one half pounds! Probably the most popular sport of all was the footrace. Athletes would compete on a track about 200 feet (60 meters).

The festival of the Olympic Games was held every four years in the sanctuary of Zeus. At the end of the games, which lasted for seven days, there was a procession and banquet. The winners of the events were considered heroes.

Project

Have fun pretending a frisbee is an ancient Grecian discus.

Materials

- Frisbees
- Aluminum foil
- Permanent marker
- Targets such as traffic cones or chalk circles drawn on the pavement
- Measuring tape

Directions

1. Cover frisbee with foil. Copy the letters onto the "discus" with permanent marker using the illustration below as a guide.

2. Take turns throwing the discus. See who can throw it the farthest. Another game is to try and aim the frisbee to land as close as possible to a target.

Coins

Historical Aid

Before the 7th century B.C., the Greeks did not use money. Instead, they used a system of barter, exchanging goods instead of buying them. The earliest money was an iron spit or skewer called an *obol*. Over time, these small rods were replaced with coins. The first coins were made in silver, but later coins were minted in gold.

The ore to make the coins was extracted from deep mines underground. Since this was difficult and dangerous work, most of the miners were slaves. The ore was refined by metal smelters and smiths before being sent to be minted. The coins were made by placing a piece of metal on an anvil between two molds. The worker struck the coin by hitting hard with a metal hammer. The edges were trimmed off. Drachmas had a picture of the goddess Athena on one side and her sacred bird on the other side. The word drachma means "bundle of spits".

Project

The first coin minted in mainland Greece were the Aegina tortoises. Make a replica of this early coin.

Directions

1. Remove the crusts from the bread.

2. Tear the bread into pieces and place in a bowl with the glue. Add a few drops of both black and white paint to make the dough silver colored. Knead until no longer sticky.

3. Form mixture so that it resembles a coin. Add detail of a tortoise and its shell with a toothpick. Let dry.

Materials

- Two slices stale white bread
- Two tablespoons (29.6 ml) white glue
- Black and white poster paint
- Newspaper
- Bowl
- Toothpick

Alphabet

Historical Aid

Our word for alphabet comes from the names of the first two letters of the Greek alphabet: alpha and beta. Most of the alphabets of modern Europe are based on the Greek alphabet. Greek letters were made of mostly straight lines. This is because most of the writing was done on tablets made of wax. The letters were scratched into the wax with a pointed tool called a *stylus*.

Older writing might be made top to bottom, left to right or bottom to top. Early Greek scribes wrote left to right until the end of a line and then came back from right to left on the next line. They called this *boustrophedon* or "turning like an ox plowing a field". Later, Greeks decided to write from the left to the right as we still do today. All letters were capitalized with no space between words and no punctuation!

Project

Practice writing the letters of the Greek alphabet. Write a message for a friend to decode using capital English letters.

Materials

• Copy of Greek alphabet chart, below, for each student or copy alphabet to the chalkboard
• Pencil   • Paper

Directions

1. Practice copying the letters of the Greek alphabet.

2. Write a message in the style of the ancient Greek scribes. Write in capital English letters. Start at the bottom right corner of the paper and write to the left. On the next line, write left to right. Do not leave spaces between the words and do not use any punctuation. Trade messages with a friend and see how long it takes to decode.

	The Greek Alphabet		
A	alpha	N	nu
B	beta	Ξ	xi
Γ	gamma	O	omicron
Δ	delta	Π	pi
E	epsilon	P	rho
Z	zeta	Σ	sigma
H	eta	T	tau
Θ	theta	Y	upsilon
I	iota	Φ	phi
K	kappa	X	chi
Λ	lambda	Ψ	psi
M	mu	Ω	omega

Language

Historical Aid

The Greek language was in use for centuries before written records were kept. Prehistoric people who migrated to Greece from Asia developed different dialects. Because Athens became the center of art and politics, the language used there became the chief language used throughout ancient Greece.

This ancient Greek language differs in several ways from the language spoken in Greece today, but the printed alphabet is almost unchanged from the ancient letters.

Many of the words we use in English are borrowed from the Greek. Artists, scientists and doctors might be surprised to learn how much Greek they know!

Project

Learn a few words in the ancient Greek language.

Directions

1. Reproduce the page "Greek Words" on card stock.

2. Have the students color and cut apart the cards. Each card provides the Greek spelling in all capital letters and the pronunciation.

3. Write the English word for the picture on the back of the card. Refer to the answer key, below.

4. The students can practice memorizing the words with the help of these flashcards. It's fun to practice with a friend.

Materials

- Card stock
- Greek words and translations, following
- Colored pencils
- Scissors

Answer Key

1. mother	7. large
2. tree	8. day
3. book	9. father
4. earth	10. world
5. small	11. friend
6. house	12. letter

1. ΜΗΤΗΡ — **MAY tayr**

2. ΔΕΝΔΡΟΝ — **DEHN drohn**

3. ΒΙΒΛΙΟΝ — **bihb LEE ohn**

4. ΓΗ — **gay**

5. ΜΙΚΡΟΣ — **mee KROHS**

6. ΟΙΚΙΑ — **oy KEE ah**

7. ΜΕΓΑΣ — **MEH gahs**

8. ΗΜΕΡΑ — **hay MEH rah**

9. ΠΑΤΗΡ — **pah TAYR**

10. ΚΟΣΜΟΣ — **KOHS mohs**

11. ΦΙΛΟΣ — **FEE lohs**

12. ΓΡΑΜΜΑ — **GRAHM mah**

Poetry

Historical Aid

Ancient Greek authors enjoyed writing many types of poetry. A favorite style of poetry was the epic poem. These poems are long and tell of the adventures of heroes and divine beings.

The greatest Greek poet was Homer, who wrote two famous epic poems, the *Iliad* and the *Odyssey*. The Iliad tells the story of the Trojan war and the heroic deeds of Greek and Trojan soldiers like Achilles and Hektor. The Odyssey continues the story with the return home of one Greek soldier named Odysseus. It took him ten years to get home with many adventures along the way. These poems taught history, geography and religious education as well as lessons in bravery. Schoolboys often recited from these poems at festivals.

Project

After listening to the story of the Trojan horse described in the Iliad, have the students draw what they think the horse looked like.

Materials

• Story of the Trojan Horse
• Paper
• Crayons or colored pencils

Directions

1. Read the story to the right of the Trojan Horse based on the epic poem, the Iliad, by Homer.

2. Draw a picture of what the Trojan horse might have looked like. Ask these questions before beginning the design: How did the Greek soldiers get into the horse? How did they breathe? How did they get out of the horse without being heard?

The Story of the Trojan Horse

For ten long years, the Greeks tried to capture the city of Troy. The soldiers became tired and wanted to return home to their families. They decided to trick the Trojans to make them surrender. They built a giant, hollow, wooden horse and filled it with soldiers. The Greek armies sailed away leaving the horse behind. A Greek spy named Sinon persuaded the Trojans to take the horse into the city. He told them the horse was magic and would keep them from harm. The horse was brought into Troy and the citizens went to bed thinking they were safe, thanks to the magical horse. During the night, however, Sinon let out the armed troops hiding in the horse. The soldiers overpowered the guards and let in the remaining Greek troops who had snuck back from the ships in the darkness. A fierce battle followed, but Troy was captured and the city burned.

Aesop's Fables

Historical Aid

Aesop was a Greek slave who lived about 600 B.C. It is believed that he wrote a collection of fables featuring animals that talk and act like human beings. A fable is a brief tale that teaches a lesson or offers advice.

One of Aesop's most popular fables is the story of *The Tortoise and the Hare*. The hare is so confident that he will win the race that he stops for a nap. The slow but steady tortoise keeps right on plodding along and not only passes the sleeping hare, but wins the race. This story teaches that persistence can be more valuable than speed.

The story of the *Ant and the Grasshopper* teaches the importance of hard work and planning ahead. When winter comes, the hard-working ant has plenty to eat, but the grasshopper who spent the summer playing starves when winter comes.

Project

Perform one of Aesop's fables in a play.

Directions

1. Divide students into groups.

2. Give groups time to read their fable. Allow each group to assign students within the group to act out the characters in the fable.

3. Groups take turns performing their play for the other groups.

Materials

• Reproduce copies of Aesop's fables, one for each group (obtain from your local library)

Some of Aesop's Fables

The Ant and the Grasshopper
The Shepherd Boy and the Wolf
The Dove and the Ant
The Hare and the Tortoise
The Lion and the Mouse
The Crow and the Pitcher

Mathematics

Historical Aid

The greatest mathematicians in the ancient world were the Greeks. Pythagoras was a mathematician who lived during the 6th century B.C. He formed a community in Italy where students could study philosophy and the relationships between numbers. He developed many mathematical theories including one about the relationship of the sides of a right triangle. Students today still study this proposition called the Pythagorean Theory.

Euclid studied astronomy, geometry, arithmetic, music and harmony at the Academy in Athens. He was invited by the king of Egypt, Ptolemy, to teach at his famous "Musaeon" or University of Scholars at Alexandria. Here Euclid studied and wrote his Thirteen Books of Elements. Much of the material deals with geometry and includes the Pythagorean Theory.

Project

Test some math theories that were proposed by Euclid and Pythagoras.

Materials

- Paper
- Pencil
- Twenty-five poker chips
- Ancient Greek Math Sheet, following

Directions

1. Reproduce one copy of the Math Sheet for each student.

2. Allow the students time to try the mathematical questions.

Answer Key

Part I	Part II
1. even	1. 9
2. even	2. 16
3. odd	3. 25
4. even	4. 25
5. odd	5. Yes
6. even	6. 5
7. odd	
8. even	
9. odd	

Math Sheet

1. A sum of even numbers is _____.

2. A sum of an even number of odd numbers is _____.

3. A sum of an odd number of odd numbers is _____.

4. If you subtract an even number from an even number, the answer will be _____.

5. If you subtract an odd number from an even number, the answer will be _____.

6. If you subtract an odd number from an odd number, the answer will be _____.

7. If you subtract an even number from an odd number, the answer will be _____.

8. If you multiply an odd number by an even number, the answer will be _____.

9. If you multiply an odd number by an odd number, the answer will be _____.

Part II. Use poker chips to study the Pythagorean Theory.

1. Multiply the length of the shortest side by itself. _____

Arrange that number of poker chips in three rows along the shortest side.

2. Multiply the length of the next longest side by itself. + _____

Arrange that number of poker chips in four rows along that side.

3. Add these two numbers together. = _____

Pythagoras says the sum of these two numbers will equal the length of the longest side multiplied by itself.

4. Multiply the longest side by itself. Longest side x longest side = _____

5. Are the two numbers the same? _____

You should be able to arrange all the poker chips in five rows along the longest side.

6. How many poker chips will be in each row? _____

3 inches

5 inches

4 inches

Science

Historical Aid

Archimedes was the greatest mathematician, engineer and physicist of ancient times. One of his engineering inventions was a water-removing device called a *cochlias*. This device, called the Archimedean Screw, is still used in Egypt today!

One day, the king of Syracuse asked Archimedes to find out if his crown was made of solid gold. Archimedes decided to take a bath and think about the problem. As he lowered himself into the bath, the water rose and spilled over the edge. He shouted, "Eureka! I've found it!" The answer Archimedes found was that an object displaced water. He learned that the heavier an object is and the bigger an object is, the more water it will displace. Unfortunately for the goldsmith, Archimedes also learned that he had cheated the king.

Project

Conduct an experiment to test the buoyancy of solids in water.

Materials

- String
- Stone
- Spring scale
- Container of water
- Paper and pencil

Directions

1. Weigh the stone on the scale and record its weight.

2. Place the container of water on the scale. Holding the stone by the string, suspend the stone in the water. Record its weight.

3. What is the difference in the weight of the stone in and out of the water? Why is there a difference? What happens to the water when the stone is lowered into it?

Medicine

Historical Aid

The Greeks believed that illness was a punishment sent by the gods. A sick person would pray to Asclepius, the god of medicine. Shrines to Asclepius were built all over the ancient Greek world. People slept in the temples and hoped that Asclepius would come to them in a dream and tell them how to cure their illness. Priests at the shrines helped to cure people by prescribing rest, herbs and simple foods. Snakes were considered sacred in ancient Greece. A live snake was kept in all temples dedicated to Asclepius. The staff of Asclepius was entwined by a single snake and called a *caduceus*.

As well as going to a temple, people would go to the doctor. Doctors knew how to treat injuries, but not how to cure diseases. There were several schools of medicine and each had its own ideas on the best way to treat patients. Hippocrates, the most famous Greek physician, believed that with rest and plain food, a body could cure itself.

Project

Make a snake figurine, as the snake was associated with the Greek god of healing, Asclepius.

Materials

- ¾ cup soap powder
- 1 tablespoon (14.8 ml) warm water
- Large bowl
- Electric mixer

Directions

1. Mix the soap powder and water in a large bowl. Mix with an electric mixer until it resembles clay.

2. Form into a snake figurine. Let dry.

Constellations

Historical Aid

The names given by the Greeks to the constellations are the ones we still use today. These names were based on myths such as the one about Orion.

Orion was a great hunter and often boasted about his skill. This bragging made the goddess Juno angry. One day when Orion and his dogs were hunting rabbit, Juno had a scorpion sting Orion and kill him.

The physician, Asclepius, brought Orion back to life using skills he learned from snakes. The god of the dead, Hades, did not like the fact that the dead could be brought back to life! When he told his brother Zeus, of his worries, Zeus threw thunderbolts, killing both Orion and Asclepius for good. Everyone, including the hare, the scorpion, and even Asclepius' snake, was put in the sky among the stars.

Project

Identify the characters in the myth of Orion in the stars.

Materials

- Constellations, following
- Pencils

Directions

1. Reproduce a Constellation page for each student.

2. Connect the dots to find the shapes of Orion, his two dogs, the hare, the scorpion, the physician, Aesulapius, and his snake.

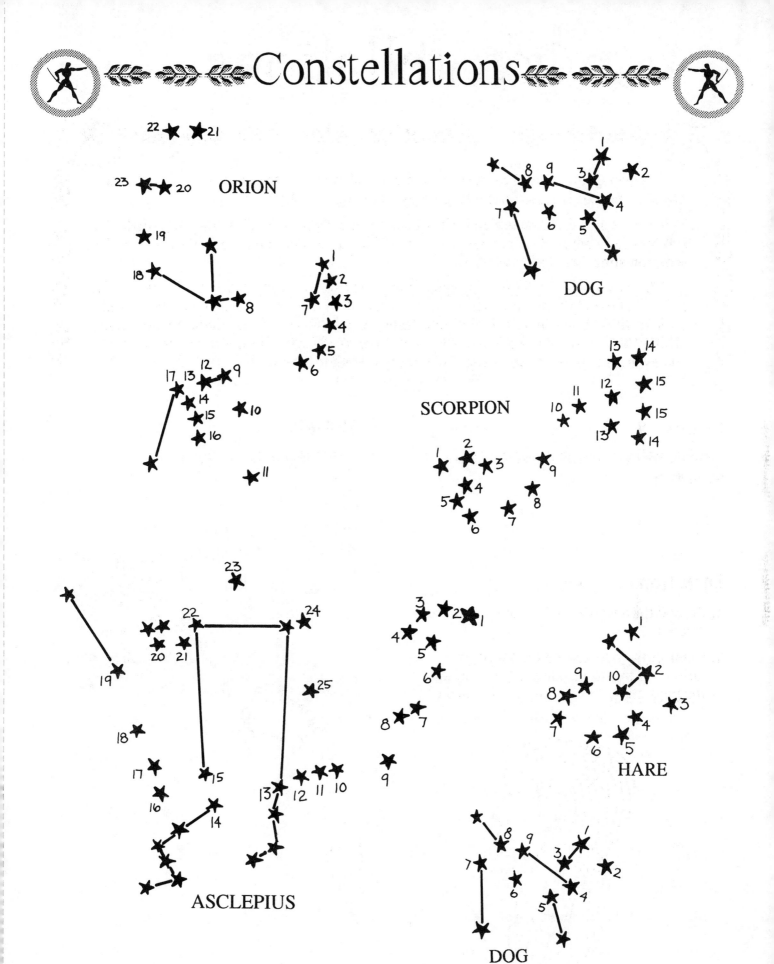

ORION

DOG

SCORPION

ASCLEPIUS

HARE

DOG

Gods and Goddesses

Historical Aid

The god and goddesses worshiped by the ancient Greeks were a lot like humans: they fell in love, married, had children and felt anger and jealousy. All gods and goddesses were descendents of Gaia (the Earth) and Uranos (the Sky). Everything that happened was willed by the gods. Zeus controlled the weather and Aphrodite made people fall in love. Demeter and her daughter, Persephone, were responsible for the harvest. Poseidon was ruler of the seas. Soldiers sought favor from Ares, the god of war. Athena was the goddess of wisdom, war and the arts.

Religion played a large part in the everyday life of the Greeks. The people spent much of their time giving thanks to the gods and warding off bad fortune. Offerings of milk, wine and cakes were made to the gods as well as animal sacrifices. Many festivals and sporting events were held to honor the gods throughout the year.

Project

Read the myth on the following page and write an original myth.

Materials

- The Myth of Arachne, following
- Paper
- Pen or pencil

Directions

1. Read a Greek myth such as the story of Arachne.

2. Write a story to explain some natural event. For example, the story of Arachne answers the question, "Where did spiders come from?" Include mythical creatures, mortals and heroes.

The Myth of Arachne

Arachne was a young maiden who became a skillful weaver. She was so talented that she became quite famous. When people came to see her work, they would gaze in awe at her beautiful designs. Even the nymphs from the streams and forests would come to watch the graceful Arachne at work. Arachne's admirers would say, "The goddess Athena must have taught Arachne herself, for no mortal girl could learn such a skill on her own."

This made Arachne quite angry as she had been taught to weave as a child by her father. Over the years, she spent many hours each day at her loom perfecting her skill. "It is through my own hard work that I have become such a wonderful weaver, not because of any help from the goddess. Besides, there is nothing that Athena could teach me, as I have become as good a weaver as Athena herself. Perhaps even better!"

One day an old woman came to watch Arachne weave. When she heard the girl's boasts, she begged her to ask forgiveness of the goddess. "Do not dare to compare yourself to the immortals," she warned Arachne, "it should be enough that you are the finest weaver among mortals."

Arachne turned to the old woman. "Why shouldn't I speak the truth," she said indignantly. "If Athena was here I would challenge her to a contest to prove that I am the most skillful weaver of all." Upon hearing these words, the old woman threw down her cane and revealed herself to be, in fact, the goddess Athena. "I accept your challenge," said Athena as she sat down at a loom.

Although she never really thought that the goddess would hear of her boasts, Arachne took her place at her loom and the contest began. People gathered from all over to watch the weavers at work. Arachne threw the shuttle from hand to hand between the threads, but as fast as she worked, Athena was just a little faster. A picture soon formed on Athena's loom, a picture that was a last warning to Arachne to repent and ask forgiveness for her pride and boasting. When Arachne saw the goddess' work, she became even angrier! As the crowd looked on in amazement, Arachne wove her bright threads into a pattern of scenes that showed the gods as evil deceivers who often played cruel tricks on their mortal servants.

As soon as Athena noticed what Arachne had done, she tore Arachne's work into bits. "You have insulted me and all the gods," raged Athena, "and such wickedness shall not go unpunished." Then she touched Arachne and said, "Live on and spin, and your descendents, too. Anyone who sees you will be reminded that it is not wise to anger Athena." At those words, Arachne's body began to shrivel and distort before the horrified watchers and she was transformed into a spider. All spiders descend from Arachne. They spin and weave their fine thread and remind mortals of the foolishness of Arachne.

Housing

The Greeks lived in houses made of sun-dried mud bricks with thatched or tiled roofs. Houses had small windows placed high on the outside wall. The rooms opened onto a central courtyard which was the main living area of the home. Here is where the family's altar to Zeus was kept. This is also where the family ate, sat and slept in good weather.

The number of rooms depended on how wealthy the family was. Women had their own separate apartments called the *gynecaeum*. This area included a room where the weaving looms and yarn were kept and a room for entertaining guests. The men of the household entertained in a dining room called the *andron*. Other rooms included the kitchen, bedrooms, bathroom and the slaves' rooms. Often, a craftsman would have his workshop in the room facing the street.

Project

Students pretend to be an architect designing a Greek home.

Materials

- Graph paper
- Pencil
- Ruler
- Colored pencils

Directions

1. Using graph paper to help make straight lines, design a Greek home. Include:

Δ courtyard   Δ men's dining room

Δ well   Δ women's rooms

Δ altar to Zeus   Δ weaving room

Δ bedrooms   Δ storage rooms

Δ slaves' rooms   Δ bathroom

Δ kitchen   Δ craftsman's workshop

2. Add details with colored pencils.

Furniture

Historical Aid

Homes in ancient Greece were not usually decorated. The walls were whitened with lime and there was little furniture. Everything from cups to lutes was hung from nails on the walls. Blankets were stored in chests and personal possessions were kept in baskets or small boxes. Tables and chairs were made of light wood and were often inlaid with ivory, gold and silver.

The man of the house sat on a large chair called a *thronos*. A smaller chair with curved legs was called a *klismos*. Most people just sat on stools that often had folding legs. Diners reclined on cushioned couches and ate from small three-legged dining tables that could be pushed under the couch when not in use. The couches used at mealtime were similar to the ones used for sleeping. They were made of wood, often decorated with bronze and had a base of leather cords. A fabric-covered mat of reeds was used as the upholstery.

Project

Think about the elements of design that Grecian craftsmen used when building storage chests and make a small, decorative box.

Materials

- Cigar box, shoebox or other small box
- Variety of materials such as pasta shapes, dried beans or shells
- Glue

Directions

1. Think about how to best arrange the selected materials to make a pleasing design. Try to use a mixture of colors and textures.

2. Apply a layer of glue to the outside of the box. Do one small area at a time. Glue the materials onto the top and sides of the box.

3. Let dry.

Symposia

Historical Aid

At night a rich Greek man might hold a banquet party for his male friends. These parties were called *symposia*. Women were not invited, but slave girls called *hetaerae* would entertain the guests. They would tell stories, sing, dance and play music. Some girls were trained to juggle and do acrobatic shows!

The evening began with a toast to the gods. The guests sat on long couches to eat and drink. Slaves would serve dishes like jellyfish, oysters, celery and dates all mixed together. There were no forks, so the food was eaten with the fingers. The diners used pieces of bread instead of napkins, then threw them to the dogs. After a night of partying, the men often played a game called *kottabos*. Each player would flick the drops of wine left in his cup at a target and bet on who would hit the mark.

Project

Taste a dessert that is similiar to one served at an ancient Greek symposia.

Directions

1. Students can grind nuts in class for an authentic experience of Greek cooking methods. It will take about 1½ cups (154.9 ml) shelled nuts to make ½ cup (118.3 ml) ground nuts. To grind nuts, you'll need a big wooden bowl and a fist-sized stone. Scrub stone thoroughly with soap before using it to break up and pulverize nuts.

2. Cream butter by beating it with spoon until fluffy and light in color. Add honey gradually, beating well after each addition. Gradually add farina, cinnamon and nuts.

3. Place in a greased cake pan. Bake at 350° F (174.9° C) for thirty-five minutes. Cool for fifteen minutes.

4. While cake is baking, make syrup by boiling honey and water together for ten minutes. Pour over cooled cake. Cool cake completely.

5. Cut into diamond shapes. Makes 16 pieces.

Materials

- ½ cup (118.3 ml) butter
- ⅔ cup (157.7 ml) honey
- 1 cup (236.6 ml) farina
- ½ teaspoon (2.45 ml) ground cinnamon
- ½ cup (118.3 ml) ground almonds
- Eight-inch (20 cm) square cake pan
- Measuring cups and spoons
- Large bowl
- Big wooden spoon
- Saucepan
- Two eggs
- Hot pads

Syrup

- 1 cup (236.6 ml) honey
- ½ cup (118.3 ml) water

Clothing

The clothing worn by the ancient Greeks was similar in shape for both men and women and changed little in design for hundreds of years.

The basic dress was a straight tunic called a *chiton* (ki´-ton). Made from a single rectangle of cloth, a chiton was cut into two pieces, pinned at intervals from the neck to the elbow and gathered at the waist with a belt. Another piece of material might be draped over the top to make a cloak called a *himation* (hi mat´e on). Workmen, soldiers and boys wore their tunics short while women, girls and older men wore a longer style.

The bright colors favored by the Greeks were created with dyes made from certain plants, sea snails and insect larva. Clothing was often edged with a colorful stripe or with a "key" pattern.

Project

Experience wearing clothing similar to that worn by the ancient Greeks.

Materials

- Large pieces of fabric or old, solid color sheets or large paper tablecloths
- Scissors
- Crayons
- Safety pins or pins made from directions on pages 10-11

Directions

1. Cut fabric into two lengths as long as the wearer is tall and about 36 inches (90 cm) wide. Cut additional fabric into long strips for belt and headband.

2. Decorate the hem in a key pattern with a crayon.

3. To wear: Pin the two pieces of fabric together at the shoulders and at intervals down the sleeves. Tie with a belt. Belts were worn high or at the waist depending on the current fashion. Sometimes two belts were worn with the fabric gently pulled out a bit between them.

4. Make a headpiece by tying a fabric strip around the head. Girls may wish to crisscross their headband or make a headdress from the directions on pages 34-35.

Headdresses

Historical Aid

The participants at religious festivals often wore wreaths made from vines on their heads. Speakers at the Assembly in Athens wore headdresses made of myrtle when they addressed their audience. Beautiful gold wreaths and sprays decorated the heads of many of the statues of gods and goddesses. The only prize given at the Olympics was a simple wreath of wild olive leaves. Wreaths were even placed on the heads of corpses in tombs.

Wreaths were not the only type of headdress worn in ancient Greece. Hairstyles were very elaborate and women often wore a gold or fabric headband. Elaborate crowns called *diadems* were made from the gold brought back from Persia by the troops of Alexander the Great. Men, too, wore headbands or golden circlets in their hair. For traveling, however, a man might wear a wide-brimmed hat called a *petasos*. It could be made of wool, fur or straw and it protected him from the sun.

Project

Make one or more of the many types of headdresses worn by the ancient Greeks.

Materials

- Tagboard
- Green chenille sticks
- Scissors
- Green construction paper
- White tissue paper
- Gold paint
- Glue
- Bobby pins
- Patterns, following

Directions

Vine Wreath

1. Trace the leaf pattern onto tagboard and cut out. Trace onto construction paper and cut out many leaves.

2. Cut chenille sticks into six-inch (15 cm) lengths. Glue a leaf to each stem. Twist two stems together. Keep adding one stem at a time to make a vine. Form the vine into a circle and twist together.

3. Cut tissue paper into small squares and crush to make myrtle blossoms. Glue to the myrtle wreath.

Golden Diadem

1. Cut tagboard to fit head in the shape shown below. A diadem is like a tiara in that it does not go all the way around the head.

2. Cut foil into long strips about three inches (7.5 cm) wide. Gently crush the foil and roll between the hands to make long twists. Wrap the foil twists around the front part of the diadem, keeping the twists close together. Cover the side pieces with foil.

3. Paint gold and let dry. Use bobby pins to attach diadem to head.

Diadem Pattern

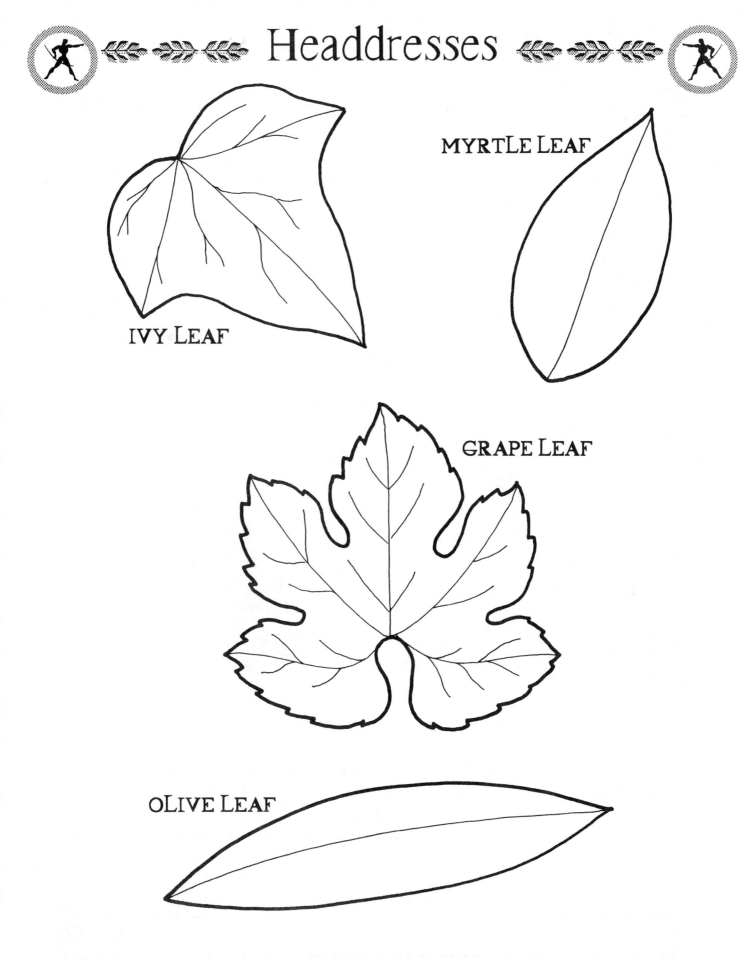

MYRTLE LEAF

IVY LEAF

GRAPE LEAF

OLIVE LEAF

Cosmetics & Perfume

Historical Aid

Greek women enjoyed using cosmetics and perfumed oils. Perfume was imported from Corinth and Rhodes in colorful glass jars or clay pots. A woman would use a special jar called a *pyxis* to hold her powder and cosmetics. These lidded jars were round and flat and made from clay. They were often painted with domestic scenes such as women spinning and weaving. Using cosmetics was only part of a Greek woman's skin care. Girls and women were careful to keep out of the sun because a suntan was considered unattractive.

After exercising, men would rub their bodies with oils to keep their skin supple. They would remove the excess oil with a curved bronze body scraper. Men were known to use perfumes as well. The fierce warriors of Sparta perfumed their long hair before going into battle.

Project

Make a pyxis or ancient Grecian cosmetic jar.

Materials

- Empty 12 oz. (360 ml) tuna can
- Patterns, following
- Scissors
- Colored pencils (authentic colors would be rust, black and light and dark beige)
- Tagboard
- Pencil
- Glue
- Tape

Directions

1. Copy one pattern sheet for each student.

2. Use the handle pattern to cut a handle from tagboard. Color and fold on dotted line.

3. Color and cut out the jar and lid patterns. Use tape to attach the two parts of the jar pattern into one long strip.

4. Mount the lid pattern onto the cardboard and trim around the edge. Carefully cut a slit in the center of the lid. Insert handle and tape.

5. Wrap the jar pattern around can and tape.

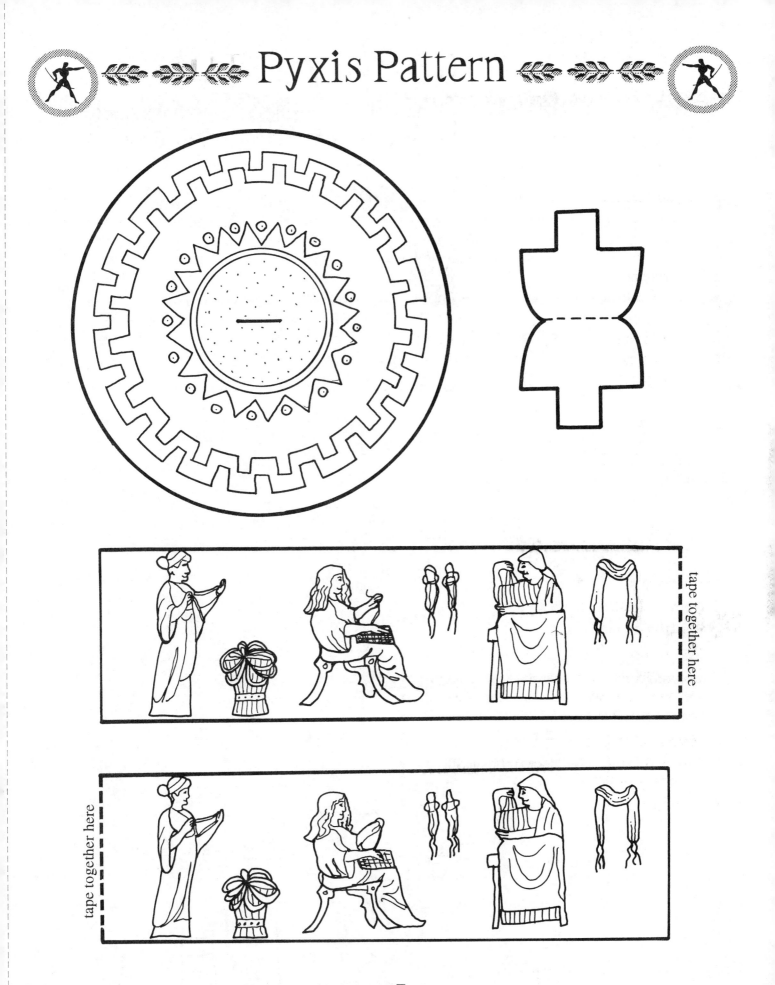

Jewelry

Historical Aid

Wealthy women owned jewelry, much of it in gold and silver. Many women had pierced ears and wore very ornate earrings. Coral, agate, amber and carnelians were often set in gold to make elaborate pins and necklaces. Bangles made with animal heads were popular in ancient Greece and were probably worn by both men and women. Rings were often set with colorful stones and sometimes the stones were carved with tiny pictures.

Beautiful jewelry was made using the technique called granulation. Artists would decorate the surface of a piece of jewelry by grouping tiny granules of gold into triangles to form an intricate design. This style of jewelry was made popular by Mycenaean craftsmen in the 1300s B.C.

Project

Make a bracelet to learn about the granulation technique used by ancient craftsmen.

Directions

1. Cut the tagboard into a strip about 3 x 8 inches (7.5 x 20 cm).

2. Draw a design of triangles onto the tagboard. Fill in the triangles with glue. Sprinkle the pastina over the glued area or arrange in rows within the triangle. Let dry. Paint with gold paint.

3. Bend into a circle. Glue or staple into a bracelet.

Materials

- Tagboard
- Pencil
- Scissors
- Glue or stapler
- Tiny pasta such as egg pastina
- Gold paint

© EDUPRESS

Music

Historical Aid

Music was an important part of life in ancient Greece. Greeks sang songs at weddings, births and funerals. They also sang many love songs, drinking songs and songs of thanksgiving to the gods. Poetry was often recited to music. There were battle songs as well, and the music from pipes kept rowers and foot soldiers on the march in time with each other.

Greek musicians played string instruments like the harp and the lyre. The soundbox of a lyre was made from an empty tortoise shell! A *kithara* is a larger wooden version of a lyre. It was plucked with a plectrum which is very similar to a modern guitar pick. Cymbals and drums were popular, as well as wind instruments like the auloi or double pipes and the syrinx. Syrinx, or panpipes, were made of reeds of different lengths and were named for the nymph, Syrinx, who turned herself into a reed.

Project

Make a set of panpipes to learn about one type of instrument played in ancient Greece.

Materials

- Tagboard
- Ruler
- Glue
- Colored pencils or crayons
- Drinking straws
- Scissors

Directions

1. Cut the tagboard into a long narrow rectangle about 2 x 10 inches (5 x 25 cm). Decorate one side.

2. Glue the straws to the tagboard as shown in the illustration. Space them about ½ inch (1.27 cm) apart.

3. Fold the tagboard over the straws and glue. Trim the longer ends of the straws so that each one is a little shorter than the one next to it.

TO PLAY: Hold the panpipes so the straws point downwards. Blow across the tops of the straws rather than into them.

Food

The Greeks ate simply. Breakfast and lunch were light meals of bread dipped in wine and water followed by dried figs, olives and perhaps some goat's milk cheese. The main meal of the day was eaten in the late afternoon or early evening and was often a barley porridge and some vegetables such as cabbage, peas, carrots or onions. Food was eaten raw, boiled or roasted. Bay leaves, garlic and oregano provided the seasoning. A wealthy family's main meal might also include fish, nuts and cheese in honey. People seldom ate meat except at religious festivals. Honey was the only sweetener available.

The Greeks were excellent bakers and made a variety of different kinds of breads, rolls and cakes. They were the first to put unusual flavorings and seeds such as poppy and sesame seeds into their bread. The Greeks are credited with making the first toast!

Project

Prepare and serve a typical dinner enjoyed in ancient Greece.

Directions

1. Bread needs to be made ahead or pita bread can be substituted.

2. Assign students to make the stew, prepare the salad and set up the buffet.

3. Set up the buffet by pushing several desks together and cover with tablecloth. Arrange vegetables in a bowl or a terra-cotta saucer for the centerpiece. For dessert serve an assortment of walnuts, almonds, dates, apples, grapes and figs arranged on serving dishes or terra-cotta saucers. Set out plates, silverware and cups. Pour juice.

Materials

- Ingredients for recipes, following
- Cutting boards
- Measuring cups, spoons
- Large bowls
- Large spoons
- Plates, silverware
- Knives
- Napkins
- Cups
- Grape juice
- Nut crackers
- Hot pads

Decorations: (Optional)

- Brightly colored tablecloth
- Assortment of vegetables enjoyed in ancient Greece such as parsnips, cabbage, lettuce, carrots, onions, garlic
- Terra-cotta serving dishes (planter saucers work well)

Greek Recipes

Preparation:

Heat oil in electric skillet. Sauté barley, onion, garlic, carrots and celery in olive oil for a few minutes. Add chicken broth and cover. Cook over lowest possible heat for 25 to 45 minutes until barley has absorbed broth.

BARLEY STEW

- ¼ cup (59.15 ml) olive oil
- 2 cups (437.2 ml) pearl barley
- 1 large onion, minced
- 1 cup (236.6 ml) chopped carrots
- 1 cup chopped celery
- 1 clove garlic minced
- 6 cups (1419.6 ml) boiling chicken broth
- Electric skillet
- Large spoon

GREEK SALAD

- Onion, sliced very thin and separated into rings
- Cabbage, shredded as for coleslaw
- Oregano, whole and crushed by hand, if possible
- Feta cheese
- Greek olives
- Olive oil
- Large bowl
- Mixing spoons

Preparation:

Combine onion, cheese, olives, shredded cabbage and oregano in a large bowl. Toss with olive oil. This salad can be made ahead and marinated for about an hour.

Preparation:

1. Mix water and milk in a bowl. Sprinkle yeast on top and dissolve.

2. Add sugar, oil, salt and three cups (709 ml) flour. Beat with electric mixer on high for ten minutes. Stir in remaining flour and knead for ten minutes.

3. Cover with a large inverted metal bowl and let rise until double. Punch down. Allow to rise a second time and punch down.

4. Divide in half. Form dough into two doughnut shapes about 13" (33 cm) across. Place on a cookie sheet that has been sprinkled with cornmeal. Brush tops of loaves with milk and top with sesame seeds. Bake at 400° F (202° C) for 25-30 minutes until light brown.

SESAME SEED BREAD

- 1 cup (236.6 ml) lukewarm water
- 1 cup lukewarm milk
- 2 envelopes fast acting dry yeast
- 2 tablespoons (29.6 ml) sugar
- 2 tablespoons oil
- 8½ cups (2011 ml) flour
- 1 teaspoon (4.9 ml) salt
- ¼ cup (59 ml) milk
- ½ cup (118.3 ml) sesame seeds
- Cornmeal
- Electic mixer
- Large bowl
- Cookie sheets
- Large spoon

Games and Toys

If a child from ancient Greece was to join a modern class at recess, he or she would have no trouble recognizing the games being played! Greek children played on swings, and enjoyed many types of ball games including a hockey-type game played with curved sticks. Children's toys included tops and yo-yos and soft leather balls stuffed with bran and used for juggling. Hoop games were popular as well as hopscotch and a game similar to jacks was played with the knucklebones from animals. Babies played with rattles and girls played with clay dolls, some with hinged arms and legs.

Adults enjoyed game-playing as well. Soldiers would often play board games while taking a break from fighting. They played games similar to chess and backgammon. The modern game of Chutes and Ladders is very similar to a game of snakes and ladders played in ancient times.

Project

Have a game day featuring some of the games enjoyed by children of ancient Greece.

Directions

1. Make the game board, tops and juggling balls on the following page or have the students bring these toys from home.

2. Set up an area for each of the games to be played.

3. Rotate the students through the stations so everyone gets a chance to play.

Materials

- Yo-yos
- Hula hoops
- Chalk
- Small stones
- Jacks
- Tops
- Game of snakes and ladders
- Juggling balls

HOPSCOTCH

Materials: chalk, stones, playground or sidewalk

Directions:

1. Draw a hopscotch court on the pavement, as illustrated. Make each square about one foot square ($.0929 \text{ m}^2$).

2. Each player gets one stone. The first player tosses stone onto number one, hops over square landing on square number two. Only one foot can be on a square at a time and feet can't touch the lines.

3. Hop square to square to ten and back again. Stop at square two and pick up stone in square one. Hop over square one. If successful, player continues tossing his stone into square two this time. Player continues until a toss is missed, a foot touches the line or two feet land in a square.

4. The winner is the first one to successfully get through all numbers.

Games & Toys

JUGGLING BALLS

Materials: fabric, scissors, needle, thread, uncooked rice or beans

Directions:

1. Cut fabric into six circles. Place two circles right sides together. Stitch almost all the way around leaving an opening about 1" (2.54 cm) wide. Turn right side out. Fill with rice and stitch closed. Repeat to make a set of three.
2. Practice tossing one ball back and forth from one hand to another. Graduate to two balls. Hold one ball in each hand. Toss one ball in the air the way you practiced. When ball reaches halfway point between hands, toss the second ball. Practice a lot. When this step is mastered, add third ball and you're juggling!

TOPS

Materials: pencils, rubber bands, wooden spools, plastic lids, jar lids, cardboard circles, nails

Directions:

1. Experiment with different materials to make a spinning top.
2. A pencil pushed through an empty sewing spool or a plastic lid can be made to spin. Hold the lid or spool in place with rubber bands and adjust the height on the pencil to get a good spin.

HOOPS

Materials: two hula hoops, cones, a chair or chalk to mark turning point

Directions:

1. Play a relay race with hoops. The hoops children of ancient Greece played with were made of wood, but a hula hoop will work just as well.
2. Form two teams.
3. Players push the hoop around the turning point and back to the next teammate. If the hoop falls over, the player must go back to the start and try again. First team whose players successfully roll their hoop around the turning point and back is the winner.

SNAKES AND LADDERS

Materials: tagboard, ruler, pencil, crayons, markers or colored pencils, dice, buttons or bottle caps to use as markers

Directions:

1. Cut cardboard into a 12" (30 cm) square. Draw a 1" (2.54 cm) border around the game board. Mark inner square into 1" blocks. Draw on snakes and ladders as illustrated. Color and label the START and FINISH squares.
2. To play: First player rolls dice and moves that number of squares. Those who land on a ladder, move up the ladder to the square at the top of the ladder. When landing on a snake, player slides down to the square at the end of the snake. The winner is the first player to reach the finish.

Ancient Greece Activity Book   **43**   © EDUPRESS

Sculpture

The Greeks created some of the greatest sculpture known. Unlike Egyptian sculptors, Greek artists created figures that were graceful and lifelike.

Gods, goddesses and athletes were favorite subjects. Artists often sculpted their male models draped only in a cloak to make them look more noble.

A famous Greek sculptor named Pheidias was chosen to make the great statue of Athena that stood inside the Parthenon. The statue stood over thirty-nine feet tall! Athena was carved from ivory plates affixed to a wooden frame and was dressed in a robe of gold. Her eyes were jewels and her wrists and waist were wreathed with snakes. She carried a massive shield and spear and had a giant snake at her side. On her head was a helmet crowned with golden horses.

Project

Greek sculptors were able to carve marble to look like draped fabric! Experiment with papier-mâché to make a sculpture.

Materials

- Newspaper
- Masking tape
- Tagboard
- White glue
- White muslin fabric scraps
- Scissors
- Tempera paint
- Brushes

Directions

Follow the directions on the following page to make a sculpture of Athena, the Greek goddess of wisdom, war and the arts.

1. Cut the tagboard as shown and form into a cone. Tape closed.

2. Crush a piece of newspaper into a ball and tape to the top of the cone. Roll a half sheet of newspaper into a tight roll and bend in half. Tape to the cone to make arms.

3. Cut hand shapes from tagboard and tape to the ends of the arms.

4. Mix two parts white glue to one part water. Cut newspaper into long strips.

5. Dip the strips into the glue and water mixture. Run the pieces between the fingers to remove the excess glue. Lay over the form, forming shoulders, the rest of the figure and facial features. Make hair attaching paper curls to head.

6. Cut two squares of fabric about the height of the figure. Dip in glue mixture and gently squeeze out excess. Drape over figure to form *chiton* (see Clothing, page 33).

7. Let dry. This may take a day or two.

8. Because Greek statues were painted, apply tempera paint to desired areas.

Pottery

Historical Aid

The Greeks were excellent potters. Some of the finest vases and jars were made in the potter's quarters in Athens known as the *Keramikos*. When the clay was put into the kiln and fired, it turned a reddish-brown color. The craftsmen learned that they could paint on their pots with gel made from very fine clay mixed with water. During the firing process, this clay "paint" would turn black.

Early Greek potters decorated their vases in the black-figure style. They painted the silhouettes of figures onto the pots before firing. After firing, the figures would turn black giving this style the name "black-figure technique". Soon after 500 B.C., the red-figure technique became popular. Now the figures were left on the red clay and the background was painted with the solution that turned black.

Project

Make a crayon resist of a Grecian amphora, or storage jar, in the red-figure style.

Materials

- Pottery Pattern, following
- Scissors
- Red-brown or golden brown color crayon
- Black watercolor paint
- Brush

Directions

1. Reproduce a copy of the jar pattern for each student.

2. Draw the outlines of a design on the jar using pencil. Scenes from favorite stories were often found on Grecian containers.

3. Color in the figures and designs with the brown crayon. Press down to leave a thick layer of crayon.

4. Paint over the entire jar with black watercolor paint. The paint will only cover the paper and the figures will remain brown! Don't worry about staying in the lines.

5. Cut out the jar.

Ancient Greece Activity Book

© EDUPRESS

Weaving

Historical Aid

Girls in Greece did not go to school. They were taught at home by their mothers to be good homemakers. They learned to look after the house and to spin and weave. Some wealthy women learned to read and write to help them keep track of the household supplies.

Weaving was practiced by all Greek women. Weaving was considered a necessary, noble art. Almost every home had a loom. In some homes, the loom was kept in the kitchen. Larger homes had an entire room for the looms and yarns.

The wool from local sheep was spun into such fine thread that Grecian garments were nearly transparent. The women also wove blankets in beautiful colors. The houses had no glass in the windows so women had to make sure they had enough blankets for winter.

Project

Learn to weave on a cardboard loom.

Materials

- Cardboard
- Ruler
- Scissors
- Yarn
- Saftey pin
- Tape
- Plastic fork

Directions

1. Cut the cardboard into a square about eight inches (20 cm) on each side. Cut notches into the top and bottom edges.

2. Tape one end of a long strand of yarn to the back of the cardboard. Wrap yarn around cardboard feeding it into the notches as you go. These threads are called the warp threads.

3. Thread the yarn through a safety pin to weave yarn strands over and under the warp threads. Use a plastic fork to push the lines of weaving close together. When you finish, turn the weaving over, cut the middle of the warp threads, remove cardboard and tie off ends.